# Crystal Healing

## *How to Use Crystals in Healing, Stress and Anxiety Management, and Development of Your Intuition*

# Table of Contents

# Thank you!

I would like to thank you for buying this book!

If you like the book and get some value out of it, after reading it, I would appreciate if you could leave a positive review on the Amazon Kindle store.

Thank you and enjoy the book!

\*\*\*

Receive e-mail updates on new book releases and free book promotions from Tabitha Zalot by signing up to the e-mail list by visiting this address: **http://bit.ly/bonus_zalot_cs**

\*\*\*

Follow us, Lean Stone Publishing, the publishing company that published this book. You will receive e-mail information on upcoming book launches, free book promotions and much more. Sign up to this e-mail list: **http://bit.ly/list_lsp_cs**

\*\*\*

Like us at **www.facebook.com/leanstonepublishing**

Follow us on Twitter **@leanstonebooks**

[3]

The trademarks that are used are without any consent, and the publication of the trademark is without permission or backing by the trademark owner. All trademarks and brands within this book are for clarifying purposes only and are the owned by the owners themselves, not affiliated with this document.

# Introduction

I want to thank you and congratulate you for buying the book *Crystal Healing: How to Use Crystals in Healing, Stress and Anxiety Management, and Development of Your Intuition.*

This book contains proven steps and strategies on how to use the unbelievable powers of these beautiful stones to improve the condition of your body and mind.

Everyone is aware of the esthetic value of crystals, in all their forms and varieties. From the oldest times, people have associated the notion of a higher social status with the possibility of wearing the rarest and most expensive jewelry. As a result, the gemstones that were the most difficult to procure have always been considered a clear symbol of wealth and affluence. Also, given their beauty and their unique aspect, crystals played an essential role in the development of the artistic world, some of them continuing to be important art forms nowadays.

But crystals are not, and have never been, appreciated only for their astonishing colors and perfect shapes. On the contrary; some of the earliest written documents attest to the metaphysical characteristics of gemstones, and that they can improve, but also potentially worsen one's physical and mental health. But, in the modern era, many scientific studies have been developed, and researchers have tried to discover the reality behind the common practice. As in any other domain, many controversial opinions emerged.

Today, the question remains: could these stones really have such an impact on our lives? If this is so, how can we explain the phenomenon and how can we use these powers for our own benefit? With so many opposite points of view, most of us do not know who is right and who isn't, having no other means at their disposal than their own experience in order to find out the truth. And for precisely this reason we decided to write this book.

Because we know that, for many of us, the truly relevant information about the crystal healing topic is not that readily available, we included in this book details that everyone should know before, during, and after using various crystals to solve some of their most ardent problems. Thus, we will give you details about some of the oldest healing practices involving crystals, we will explain some of the most common techniques, how each part of our body can be influenced by the properties of these stones, and we will focus more on what exactly we can do to take control of our stress, anxiety, and intuitive power.

What needs to be emphasized from the very beginning is that this book should not, under any circumstance, be taken as a justification for stopping any other form of medical treatment unless you have previous consent from your physician. We know that there are many voices who argue that gemstones can cure serious medical conditions (such as cancer or AIDS), but we are not one of them. Instead, we will show you how to use crystals to control your emotions, and eventually achieve the ability to be at peace with yourself and the outside world.

Read this carefully and learn how to be happy again.

Thanks again for buying this book, I hope you enjoy it!

# Chapter 1 – Ancient Practices of Crystal Healing

Before understanding the consistency and physical characteristics of these curious stones, it is important to have a general context of their usage throughout time. Crystals, like many other rare natural resources, have been valued by different populations from every corner of the world beginning in the oldest times. The uses that were attributed to these gemstones were as various as there were peoples and cultures.

Each and every one discovered a new way in which crystals could be used. Being considered as much a religious tool as, something that comes to contradict different religions, gemstones have been perpetually either appreciated and searched for, or forbidden from everyday use. But, in one way or another, this practice has been preserved until our times, and it will probably be used by many generations to come. This information would not have stood the test of time if there was not a good reason.

We have probably all observed that the popular tendency is to contradict everything our parents think they know with more or less relevant scientific studies, and to suggest newer theories that keep us interested in the respective domain. We don't want to say that these studies are completely wrong or that we should stop studying them; what we want to say is that we should always check more sources before establishing our own opinion.

The purpose of paying attention to the historical background of crystal healing is acknowledging the fact that this practice is thousands of years old, each generation taking the best from their ancestors. And the most astonishing thing is that more or less similar metaphysical properties of crystals have been observed at different times by completely different populations, who had no possibility of communicating between them. But let us observe, point by point, how some of these ancient cultures used precious stones in their medical and spiritual practices.

## Greek Culture

The ancient Greeks used crystals in a wide variety of practices, attributing to them many beneficial properties that have been preserved until present times. Even the word *crystal* is considered to come from the Greek term *krustullos*, which would literally translate to *ice*, because the common perception of the time was that crystals were heavenly forms of frozen water sent by gods. And because they never defrost, it was considered that they can transmit this permanent state of force and power to human beings. This is why many Greek men would always have a crystal amulet with them in order to keep them safe.

Other more specific uses included amethysts – a word related to the Greek term for *sober* – that would keep individuals away from drunkenness, and hematite stones, which got their name because of the red color that is obtained when it oxidizes. Being an iron ore, hematite was also associated with Aries, the god of war. This is why crushed hematite would be rubbed on the soldiers' bodies before going to war to give them strength and invincibility.

## The Roman Empire

The same important role of keeping their soldiers safe in battles was attributed by early Romans to different crystal amulets and charms. Even though they would later be banned by the church, crystals continued to be considered a way to protect people's health, wealth, and to keep bad spirits away.

## Chinese Culture

The most common form of crystal usage in the ancient Chinese culture included jade. As much for ornamental purposes, as for its incredible power to cure several diseases of the body and mind, crystals were an important segment in the history of the Chinese people. By far the most appreciated property of different precious stones was their healing power. Given their long usage in history, it is not at all surprising that today, acupuncture, another similar form of alternative medicine, is so popular in China.

## Indian Culture

Important aspects of the modern usage of crystals concerning their healing abilities – and what is to be discussed in the following chapters – comes from the ancient Indian culture. From the oldest times, crystals have been involved in Aryuvedic medicine as a way to achieve the necessary balance in people's emotions and a general peace of the mind and soul. The Vedas, which represent the oldest forms of Sanskrit literature and scriptures of Hinduism, also give specific details about the healing powers that each stone has. Some of the most important forms of crystal treatment are those dealing with inner harmony, general tranquility, wisdom, better judgment, and a well-balanced chakra.

## Ancient Egypt

Among the first to discover the healing powers of crystals were the Egyptians, who were absolutely sure that, when used correctly, they would have a beneficial effect in all their daily activities. It is believed that some of the most valued gemstones were amazonite, quartz, emerald, hematite, carnelian, fluorite, garnet, lapis lazuli, malachite, peridot, turquoise, and serpentine – all of them having their specific purposes. Even when it came to jewelry, the color of each crystal was extremely important, and it had to match the personal needs of the owner. Among the most popular ways of using crystals were: wearing them near the heart (to bring balance in that person's love life), on their forehead (to awaken the Third Eye – bringing wisdom and a general sense of awareness), or giving them to deceased people to ensure an easier passage to the afterlife.

# Chapter 2 – What Are, In Fact, Crystals?

In the previous chapter we have seen how the healing powers of crystals were discovered and made use of in different contexts by many generations before our times. Even though each of them included certain gemstones and various cultural aspects specific to them, we can easily observe the similarity between their practices. This way, it is not hard to understand why, even today, so many healing processes involve crystals.

But some of us, especially the ones who are new in this field, may still wonder: what exactly are these crystals, what are they made of, and how come they have these powers and other rocks don't? If this is also your case, then this chapter was created precisely to give you a more detailed explanation of the physical properties and characteristics of these mysterious stones.

## *The Science behind Crystals*

To put it simply, crystals (which are also known as crystalline solid) are minerals composed of atoms, ions, or molecules that form their microscopic structure. These structures are unique for every single type of crystal, and they also lead to their perfect geometrical shape (with flat faces and usually sharp angles), which allows us to identify them easily.

In charge of studying all the particularities of each stone is crystallography – the science of crystals and crystal formation in nature. Thus, the size and shape of each crystal depends on the natural conditions of the place in which it was formed, and the time it took for them to grow (some of them developing over thousands of years).

The idea behind all crystal healing practices is that crystals have the power to preserve something like a memory, to conserve a certain energy that is taken from the exterior, and that will be transmitted to everything around them. And this is how we get to the first techniques that anyone interested in this subject should know: programming and cleansing.

## Programming and Cleansing

Given their ability to preserve energies, crystals can be "charged" with a certain feeling or emotion that we want them to spread in a specific area or on another person. We can do that by holding the stone tightly in our hand, for example, while focusing our mind and soul on the specific emotion that we want the crystal to express. Of course, in order to be able to do such a thing we need to be prepared in advance, and this is why only those who have these innate capacities are recommended most often for this task.

However, in order to spread the positive energy, crystals will "collect" the negative aspects from that room or the person's mind. Thus, the stones will retain those negative emotions. For this reason, they often require cleansing – a process through which they are cleaned of all the negative elements that they have collected. And there are various cleansing techniques: they can be left for one or more nights in clean water under the moonlight, buried in a safe place for a couple of days to take the energies of the earth, or, if possible, kept for a few days in sea water. The explanation for all of these cleansing methods is that the crystals need to be connected with the natural energies of the places where they were formed – water or earth.

Of course, there are many other aspects that you need to be aware of when you want to charge or clean your crystal. The most important aspect is to know exactly what you want to use it for, because there are certain places and times of the year that have a prevalent influence on a specific energy. For example, if you want energy and vitality – you can place your crystal in sea water at high tide; if, on the contrary, you are in search of peacefulness and calmness, you should put it in sea water at low tide. Also, the time of year plays an important role: spring equinox can contribute to your overall development, summer solstice can bring you passion and happiness, autumn equinox will contribute to the fulfillment of your dreams, and winter solstice is a symbol for renewal.

## *The Importance of Shapes and Colors*

In every healing process involving crystals, the shape and color that you use are extremely important. This is why you need to pay attention to what the crystal looks like.

Possible shapes:

- Chunks (no easily observable facets) – can be used to increase the intensity of any energy from a specific area or during a certain activity

- Cut crystals (whose form was established by a human hand through polishing and cutting) – are recommended when a change is needed

- Clusters (multiple crystals naturally connected between them) – they can increase feelings such as safety or security and give a general calm atmosphere

- Single terminated (with a sharp edge) – their shape makes them appropriate to be worn as amulets that have the purpose of protecting and enlightening the mind of the owner.

Possible colors and their meanings:

- Blue – peace, early life, mysticism

- Brown – natural habitat, order, rules to be established

- Black – stability, security

- Green – life, nature, prosperity, rebirth

- Gray – maturity, distress, wisdom

- Indigo – reflection, introspection, intuition

- Orange – liveliness, active energy

- Pink – love, care

- Purple – elevated condition (being a symbol of royalty), well-being

- Red – dynamism, self-confidence, courage

- White – purity, ingenuity

- Yellow – intelligence, joyfulness, energy

# Chapter 3 – How Does Crystal Healing Work?

In the previous chapter, we focused on general information about the world of crystals, what they are, and the methods and explanations for some activities that are involved when we want to initiate ourselves in these practices. Now it is time to get more into the details and find out exactly what we need to know before actually beginning the healing processes. Let us look at the theory behind science and try to understand how we can make use of it in real life.

## What Is DOR and How Does It Affect Us?

First of all, we need to explain the concept on which a big part of the crystal healing practice is based: Dominant Oscillatory Rate or DOR to make it easier to remember. To begin with, we need to understand that absolutely everything in this world is made of vibrations. All these crystals (and stones in general) differentiate themselves through the fact that they have a permanent physical structure.

This means that each stone vibrates certain energy at a fixed rate, which is their Dominant Oscillatory Rate. We, as human beings (and animals as well, but to a much smaller extent), are made of varying DORs (due to the fact that each cell in our body has its own DOR) that can be easily influenced by any external factor. This way, we get to observe why crystals can play such an important role for us. If you know how to use them (and you will by the end of this book), their steady DOR can balance your fluctuating one. It seems simple now, isn't it?

## What Do We Understand through Vibrational Medicine?

To move on, we need to focus on that part of medicine that, for various reasons, is less known to the common population:

Vibrational Medicine and the ways in which it functions. To put it in simpler words, the human body has two major states: the one of health (when everything functions properly and in complete harmony) and the one of disease (when something has been disturbed as a cause of a wrong frequency of vibrations and energies).

And this is where vibrational medicine intervenes: it tries to recreate balance and let our body and spirit take back its normal path. As previously pointed out, the most common way to do that is by making use of the unchanging DOR of a crystal. The choice of the stone or stones that are to be used is not that easy to make because they need to have certain characteristics to meet one particular problem.

This is exactly what the upcoming chapters will present you. But crystal healing is not the only method implied by vibrational medicine: healing with light and colors, healing with herbs, with music (sound), and with the four elements of nature (air, earth, fire, water). Each of these varieties has well-established ways in which they can be applied for the healing of different mental, emotional, and physical conditions.

## *The Meaning of "Affirmation"*

As you might have imagined, the simple holding or touching of a crystal, even if it was rightly chosen, is not enough for the healing process to be complete. Our inner thoughts and, in certain cases, those of the person performing the healing on us are extremely important. And one of the most common techniques in this situation is the one of "affirmations". Affirmations are our own messages that we, consciously or unconsciously, transmit to ourselves, and which are intended to obtain a desired outcome.

In order to achieve the results that we want, we need to pay attention to the way in which we address ourselves when we face a specific situation. For example, when we experience a misfortune or something that we perceive as negative, we must avoid saying "Yes, it was entirely my fault; I am not good enough for this; I will never be able to do it properly" or "This has never worked for anyone I know; why should I even bother trying?" and many, many other similar ones. Instead, we need to turn them into positive thoughts by emphasizing what we can and what we will do to improve our situation.

This technique of affirmation needs to be done on three different levels: auditory, visual, and emotional. We need to hear ourselves say how we will accomplish whatever we want, to try to picture in our mind how we will enjoy the accomplished outcome, and to imagine what we will be feeling in those moments. And we will be able to do all of this once we get rid of all the negative emotions and thoughts that sometimes overwhelm us.

# Chapter 4 – Most Common Healing Properties

Up to this point, we have focused on the understanding of theoretical information that anyone who is interested in this topic should be aware of. But how exactly can these crystal stones actually help us? We know that everything happens on the metaphysical level, and that the actions that take place cannot be measured in the traditional way, having only the results to testify for their wonderful characteristics.

However, we need to know precisely what purposes crystal healing can be used for. Even though no gemstone has one singular area in which it can be used, tradition and common practice, that dates back to the earliest days, taught us that some of them proved to be more helpful for a certain problem. In order to find out more about what stone is to be used where, pay attention to the following classification of some of the most common properties of crystal healing.

### 1. Crystals for Concentration: Bloodstone and Citrine

These stones are mainly used for clarity of the mind, the ability to focus on a certain activity, and for the moments when you want to let go of something without suffering from depression or similar conditions. They all give you strength, self confidence, and are excellent when you need a boost of optimism and positive attitude around you.

### 2. Crystals for Energy: Opal and Topaz

These crystals differentiate themselves through their much higher vibration rates, which gives them the ability to produce a faster change in our system. For this reason they are most commonly used for the moments when you feel weak, constantly tired, and with no will to make even one more step in a certain direction. Their energy is so high that, if you keep them near your body or in your bedroom, they will also affect your sleep. And this is only their general usage; each of these stones has many variations (of colors and shapes) that can be used in a wide range of healing processes.

### 3. Crystals for Meditation: Amethyst, Lapis lazuli, Geode, Lolite and Alabaster

These crystals have the power to support a pure and successful meditation, by helping you disrupt your mind from the immediate reality, in order to connect your senses to the greater forces of nature. All of these stones have a more spiritual side, being perfect for the moments when you want to reach other levels of consciousness. Many of them can also be used for dream analysis in case of nightmares that produce disturbance, anxiety, or unrest. Another effect that these stones can have is to calm a rather agitated situation and to ease tensions.

### 4. Crystals for the Memory: Carnelian, Garnet, Ruby, and Turritella Agate

The ability to enhance memory abilities is one that, in general, characterizes most of these stones, due to their steady dominant oscillatory rate, that helps them preserve any energy for longer. This is why they are often recommended to be used as amulets in those situations when great memory is essential: either when we need to remember certain details from the past, or when we need to make sure that we will "stock" new information for the future. They also have great protection powers; they can improve the spiritual love for ourselves and for those around us, and let us receive the ups and downs of life with more calm.

### 5. Crystals for the Love Life: Apatite, Rose Quartz and Colbaltocacite

Unfortunately, for those who hoped for easy and fast help in this aspect, these crystals are not named because, in a miraculous way, they can make you fall in love instantly with a certain person or, on the contrary, enter someone else's mind and soul and make them go crazy for you. No, such practices do not represent crystal healing. What they can do, however, is to balance your energy in such a way as to be able to get over broken heart problems more easily, to increase your self esteem, love and appreciation for your own being, and to offer you the inner peace that was disturbed by several factors. Only in this way will you be able to offer and receive love again.

## 6. Crystals for Protection: Diamond, Fluorite and Yellow Jasper

Just like in the case of the crystals for memory enhancing, those that are considered to work better for giving protection can also be used for a large series of purposes. In order to be able to help us stay away from all the negative energies that we have to deal with in the course of a day, it is recommended to wear such stones as amulets very close to our body. And they work on different levels: while yellow jasper, for example, is better to be used in the outdoors to offer us physical protection, fluorite can protect our spirit and our emotions from being affected in another way. Among their other properties we can also find their ability to make our mind clearer, to give us more physical strength, and to help us discern between what is good and what is bad. Because they can preserve all the negative energies in them, they need to be cleansed more often.

## 7. Crystals for Stability: Coral, Pietersite, Bloodstone and Petrified Wood

A very well known property of crystals in general is that of "keeping our feet on the ground", of balancing our energy as to make us more focused, aware, and dedicated to one single domain, which can be a physical one or not. Even though their whole purposes depend on their color and shape, they are believed to help our mental stability, to make us more focused on our goals, and to not let us follow chimeras that don't exist.

## 8. Crystals for the Balance of Chakras: Jade, Serpentine, Fulgurite, Tourmaline, and Kyanite

Chakra balancing is considered to be the prime property of crystal stones. Aligning the energies properly on each of the seven levels, taken separately or as a whole, is essential for a complete healing. Each of these stones has a prevalent purpose and usage, being highly recommended for one problem or another. Because chakra balancing with the help of crystals is such a complex and important topic, it will be discussed in more detail in the following chapter.

# Chapter 5 – Understanding Chakras and the Seven Body Zones

In the previous chapter we have, very briefly, introduced the notion of chakra, the idea that it is essential to maintain the right balance between all the major chakras in our body, and that crystals are a great way to do that. Because not many of us are familiar with these aspects, in this chapter, we will try to understand how a well-balanced chakra can help us in the healing process. Let us take it step by step and focus on different defining elements.

## *What Do We Understand By Chakra System?*

The Sanskrit term "chakra", which literally translates to "wheel" or "turning", makes a clear reference to our inner vibrations and energies that are in perpetual movement, constantly rotating. This concept comes from old yogic and tantric practices of Buddhism and Hinduism, being founded on the idea that the human body is more than what we can see (the physical body); it is also formed by the subtle body – made by psychological and spiritual elements. Chakras are, of course, part of the subtle body, which is believed to include seven dominant regions.

These chakras are aligned along our spinal cord and reach the space from the top of our head. However, since they are not physical elements (like our organs for example), their exact location can vary. Also, each chakra has its own rotating (the symbol of the wheel) speed and, on a normal level, the speed increases as we move to the higher chakra. Furthermore, each of the seven major chakras is connected to the rest of the body on all possible levels: physical, spiritual, emotional, and mental.

## Why Is It Important to Maintain a Balanced Chakra System?

This is why, when we experience any form of energetic imbalance, our internal organs can suffer the consequences. And the way to keep them balanced is by making sure that we keep them open – that we let the energies flow through our bodies without blocking them in a certain corner of our mind. Because, if one or more of the main chakras are closed (as a consequence of a negative experience that let marks on our conscience), the meeting points of the energies will also be blocked, thus giving birth to serious conditions.

As we will see immediately, each chakra is attributed one single color: red, orange, yellow, green, blue, indigo and violet – the colors of the rainbow. And each of them can respond to the same color or its complementary color. Also, other aspects – like the age, energy level, anxiety, stress, physical, and mental development of the person – must be taken into consideration before proceeding in the process of crystal healing. In order to know what and when to use, let us find out more about the properties of each of the major seven chakras.

## Which Are the Main Chakras?

### 1. Root Chakra

**Location:** at the base of the spine in the region of coccyx perineum; it is connected with the leg, intestines, bladder, tailbone, teeth, and blood circulation

**Color:** Red, but also brown and black

**Glands and affected emotions**: Adrenals - Passions

**Functions:** it ensures the basic needs for survival, safety, and security; it can also influence one person's courage, grounding, individuality, and sexuality (for male persons)

**Possible dysfunctions:** bladder infection, problems with the sexual organs, hemorrhoids, constipation, numbness, anemia, leukemia, but also anxiety, frustration, and constant fear

**Recommended crystals:** Garnet, Black Tourmaline, Obsidian, and Smoky Quartz

## 2. Spleen Chakra

**Location:** in the lower abdomen, just below the navel; it is connected to the ovaries/testicles, the kidneys, spleen, urinary tract

**Color:** Orange

**Glands and affected emotions:** Gonads - desires

**Functions:** it can influence one's confidence, need for intimacy, sensuality, desire to procreate, sociability

**Possible dysfunctions:** sexual impotence or frigidity, STD, low libido, depression – linked to alcoholism and drug abuse, asthma, but it can also disturb your intuition, creativity, and friendliness

**Recommended crystals:** Carnelian Agate, Tiger's Eye, Orange Calcite

## 3. Solar Plexus Chakra

**Location:** solar plexus, stomach, below the breast bone; it is connected to the stomach, pancreas, liver, intestines, nervous system, diaphragm

**Color:** Yellow

**Glands and affected emotions:** Pancreas – Sense of Purpose

**Functions:** the center of personal power, self-control, awareness, will, optimism, wit, intelligence, humor, laughter

**Possible dysfunctions:** diabetes, hypo and hyperglycemia, ulcer, hepatitis, toxicity, but also depression, nervousness, low self-esteem, timidity

**Recommended crystals:** Yellow Calcite, Citrine, Topaz

### 4. Heart Chakra

**Location:** in the center of the chest, right behind the breast bone; it is connected to the heart, thymus gland, lungs, arms, and the respiratory, and circulatory systems

**Color:** Green and Pink

**Glands and affected emotions:** Thymus - Love

**Functions:** it ensures the need for love, harmony, compassion, peace, acceptance, and the general tendency to see only the good in everyone

**Possible dysfunctions:** Breathing problems, pneumonia, asthma, high blood pressure, heart problems, insomnia, but it can also make you afraid to love, and to let yourself be loved, feel unworthy, paranoid, and insecure

**Recommended crystals:** Kunzite, Tourmaline, Pink Quartz

### 5. Throat Chakra

**Location:** in the throat (near the middle of the collarbone); it is connected to the mouth, tongue, jaw, shoulders, neck and throat, vocal system

**Color:** Shades of Blue

**Glands and affected emotions:** Thyroid - Growth

**Functions:** Creative speech and forms of expression, effective communication, wisdom, confidence, and trust

**Possible dysfunctions:** High body temperature, sores, toothaches, infections, tonsillitis, hyperactivity, but also OCD, melancholy, mood swings, tendency to feel guilty, timid, or unable to express yourself

**Recommended crystals:** Azurite and Aquamarine

### 6. Third Eye Chakra

**Location:** in the forehead, right above the physical eyes; it is connected to the eyes, ears, nose, nervous system, forebrain, sinuses

**Color:** Indigo and Purple

**Glands and affected emotions:** Pituitary - Intuition

**Functions:** it affects one's intuition, imagination, understanding, self-perception, and realization, memory

**Possible dysfunctions:** migraines, sleep problems, blindness, hearing difficulties, but also paranoia, schizophrenia, depression, fear of themselves, and of others

**Recommended crystals:** Lapis Lazuli, Amethyst, Sodalite

### 7. The Crown Chakra

**Location:** at the top of the head; it is connected to the central nervous system, upper brain, cerebrum, hair growth

**Color:** Violet and White

**Glands and affected emotions:** Pineal – Spirituality

**Functions:** it affects the general sense of awareness, meditation, wisdom, wit, intuition, spiritual energy; it can give complete access to our conscious and unconscious mind

**Possible dysfunctions:** it can cause mental disorders and alienation, depression, frustration, and other destructive emotions

**Recommended crystals:** Amethyst, Clear Quartz Crystal, Oregon Opal

# Chapter 6 – How to Cure Stress with Crystals

Having to deal with different levels of stress will definitely be remembered as the "disease" that characterized the last decades of the 20<sup>th</sup> century and the beginning of the present one. How many people can actually say that they are always at peace with the way their life is going, that they have everything under control at all times, and that nothing is enough to ruin their perfect balance? Not too many, right?

But this is perfectly normal, taking into account the difficult times in which we live with all the financial, social, and environmental problems that, directly or indirectly, affect our sense of stability, security, and safety. However, a major problem arises when we see ourselves with the impossibility of getting back on the right track, and we observe ourselves caught in a perpetual circle of worries, agitation, and anger. This is when we need to act, to do something productive to improve our mental and emotional condition, in order to preserve our physical strength.

And, as we have seen in the previous chapters, certain crystals can play an important role in our stress management sessions. When we observe that we cannot control something by ourselves, it is now very common to make use of various crystal healing techniques. And why wouldn't it be, since so many incredible results have been obtained in earlier times? We just need a little documentation, a strong faith, and strong will to produce a change in our way of being.

## Most Commonly Used Crystals for Stress Healing

As we have seen when we discussed the various elements of the seven major chakras, each part of our body – both the physical body and the subtle body – is connected to various disorders that can appear once our balance is derailed, and they can be healed with one or more stones that have the necessary properties. The same is valid for the healing of stress conditions: some crystals have been observed to have a higher impact than others.

- **Amethyst** – it helps you stay focused, achieve a state of meditation, self-consciousness, and high spiritual levels, it improves your memory, thinking capacities, and the ability to easily make decisions, it can calm your agitation, anger, fury, and it offers protection against negative energies

- **Aquamarine** – it helps you clear your mind in order to see everything around you in a brighter light, it contributes to your faster understanding of things, and, as a consequence, it gives you the opportunity to have the big picture of the situation in which you are in, so that you can use it to organize your priorities and eventually come up with the solution.

- **Clear Quartz** –considered one of the most powerful crystals, clear quartz can help you improve almost every aspect of your physical, mental and emotional conditions; it is recommended because it raises the inner energy, stimulates our thinking capacities, and ensures a balance of our emotions, which is exactly what we need in order to see things straight and be able to get out of a stressful situation.

- **Fluorite** – this one is definitely essential when we have troubles organizing different aspects of our life, and classifying them according to their importance and temporary urgency – but without being biased or influenced by other factors; it is also believed to help you finally see the truth of a certain situation, so when your stress is caused by uncertainty, this stone is necessary for you.

- **Moonstone** – this stone has the magical property to calm any tense or tension filled situations, it helps you become more equilibrated in what concerns your emotions, and it can also ensure a balance between your feminine and masculine energies.

- **Rose Quartz** – its major characteristic is its ability to improve love and relationship problems between partners, but rose quartz is also recommended for protecting you against negative energies, it also encourages self-confidence, and re-establishes emotional balance.

- **Smokey Quartz** – this type of quartz is mostly recommended for people who need a little help in managing complicated situations because it gives them strength and positive energy; it is also an efficient grounding crystal that alleviates any negative emotion or dangerous tendency when the person is faced with difficult moments.

## Crystal Healing Techniques to Reduce Stress

After finding out which crystals can be used for different purposes, we also need to become familiar with some techniques that are often included in the healing process.

**Meditation** - contrary to common belief, healing through meditation is extremely simple and it can be practiced by absolutely anyone. You just need to find a quiet place, or one where you will not be interrupted by anything or anyone, lay down in a comfortable position, with your crystals in your hands or placed on the right part of your body, and just focus on the idea that everything is under control. By stopping your mind from worrying for various reasons, you will achieve the sense of peacefulness and relaxation that is so needed in such a situation.

**Affirmation** – just as it was described in the third chapter, affirmation can be effective in almost all mental and emotional healing practices. In this case, you can use the power of positive affirmations in combination with the beneficial influence of one of the previously mentioned crystals, and clear your mind of all the negative thoughts that indirectly force you to remain in this damaging stressful position; in order to be effective, this technique needs to be practiced constantly for a longer period of time.

**Wearing Them As Amulets** – in case you want even stronger and quicker results, you can wear a crystal stone so that it is always with you; this way, you make sure that you will be protected from negative energies and influences everywhere you go.

# Chapter 7– How to Cure Anxiety with Crystals

Even though stress and anxiety are often perceived as working together and affecting a person's emotional, mental, and sometimes even physical stability, their "healing" methods are not always the same. And the best way to understand why is by imagining stress as an immediate response of our body to outside factors that disturb its natural balance, and anxiety about what happens in our body and mind when the stress and problems are not resolved properly, and degenerate into more complicated conditions.

Of course, anxiety does not always happen as a result of a longer period of continuous stress and agitation; it can also appear as a later consequence of a trauma, more serious problems that have not been overcome yet, or anything else that left evident marks on one person's consciousness. And the worst part is that, in more serious cases, people that have strong anxiety issues can eventually lose control of themselves, and forget how to come back to the reality of the world in which they live.

The most common forms of manifestation are panic attacks, paranoia, constant fear, and insecurity. When this happens too often and for unknown reasons, the person needs to find help. Fortunately, it was discovered long ago (and put in practice ever since) that several crystal stones have a miraculous effect on treating people's issues related to various forms of anxiety. For minor cases, some of the crystals that were mentioned in the chapter dedicated to stress healing can also be used.

## Most Commonly Used Crystals for Anxiety Healing

Being such a delicate problem, that, in some cases, can have serious repercussions on someone's personal and professional life, it needs to be treated very cautiously and with the maximum belief in the possibility of change. The most useful crystals for this condition are:

- **Black Tourmaline** – the greatest power of this stone is that it ensures protection for the person using it, against the negative energies within themselves, and against those from the exterior; it can also increase that person's vitality and energy, which are so necessary in these rather dark periods. Because it attracts so many negative energies, it needs regular cleansing.

- **Rose Quartz** – what could be more indicated for the counterattack of negative energies, fear, constant panic, and mistrust than a crystal that has the power to enhance our love feelings for ourselves and for everything that surrounds us? And we already know that this crystal is rose quartz, which does not "attack" the emotions associated with anxiety directly, but it produces new emotions, full of optimism and positive feelings, that are strong enough to cover, reduce, and gradually eradicate anything that stops that person from feeling fulfilled.

- **Nirvana Quartz** – similar to rose quartz, nirvana quartz is helpful in these situations because it has the ability to improve one person's acceptance, understanding, and respect for his/her own being; it is truly a unique crystal in the sense that, as its name tells us, it can lift the spiritual self of the person to such a level that it gives her/him complete comprehension of the whole situation.

[33]

- **Lapis Lazuli** – this stone is almost a universal one, having he incredible ability to solve some of the most difficult and diverse mental and emotional problems; its main property is that of "opening the Third Eye", of enlightening the person's mind, and giving them the capacity to have a clearer understanding of what really matters in life; this stone also offers protection against psychic attacks, unexplainable paranoia, and constant nightmares.

- **Lepidolite** – this stone can also be used to fight against stress, especially when the person, just like in our case with anxiety, is looking for a complete change in their way of thinking, behaving, and –gradually – feeling. Being a stone of transition, this crystal can raise someone's sudden awareness of the real situation in which he/she finds him/herself, and in the process of finding inner peace and sense of self-worth; it can also calm a person, induce sleep, and equilibrate the nervous system.

- **Lithium Quartz** – this gemstone was long believed, in the ancient forms of crystal healing, to solve all the emotional problems that one person left unresolved in a previous life. Today, specialists are more reserved and only recommend it for bringing inner peace, a general state of relaxation and calmness, and for rebalancing any issue encountered by the major chakra levels.

## Crystal Healing Techniques against Anxiety

<u>Meditation</u> – of course, the most common healing technique is meditation; and it is not that difficult to understand: what could help us more than being at peace with our inner thoughts, focusing on what we need to let go before actually being able to embrace the present and the future, and seeing the bigger picture in the situation that produces so much harm? Again, this can be achieved only though complete

[34]

concentration and strong will, but, if we use the right stones, this will not be a problem.

**<u>Crystal & Scent Therapy Sessions</u>** – because treating anxiety issues refers to a more deeply rooted problem, we need to organize different sessions in which we concentrate on all our senses to obtain the desired result; for this technique you will need, again, a room to offer you privacy, an appropriate musical ambient (or complete silence if you prefer), the aromatic scent of various herbs (like lavender or your favorite essential oils), and, of course, the recommended crystal stones that you can keep in your hands or place on your body.

**<u>Wearing them as amulets</u>** – this technique should be performed at the same time as other ones in order to help you deal with your fear and panic problems wherever you are.

# Chapter 8 – How to Improve Your Intuition with Crystals

The struggle to improve one's intuitive abilities and to open the Third Eye to guide them in life has always represented a major preoccupation for anyone who was introduced to this world of tantric traditions, in which these elements play an essential role. Of course, everyone has a certain level of intuition; the problem remains in the way in which each person knows how to make use of it and, eventually, how to improve it in order to achieve more elevated levels of metaphysical knowledge.

Intuition can also be described as an inner awareness, or sense of duty that a person has a certain purpose in life, a certain direction to which he or she needs to go, and an easier understanding of what they need to do in order to accomplish their mission. Unquestionably, this ability to know how to give meaning to your life, and to know how to always make the right choices is universally desired, but, not many persons are aware of the ways in which they can cultivate it. Crystal healing is only one of the many techniques. Let us first see what types of crystals are most commonly recommended, and, then, find out how precisely we can do that.

## *Most Commonly Used Crystals to Develop One's Intuition*

In order to develop intuition with the use of crystals, we need to make sure that we use the right ones (those associated with the crown and Third Eye chakras). Because there are a large number of stones associated with the ability to improve intuition, we will include here only the most common ones:

- **Amethyst** – this stone offers, primarily, a great protective power against all negative energies, and support for mental and emotional strength and wisdom; also, the amethyst allows access to the higher levels of spirituality, thus letting you obtain forms of knowledge that are not normally available to the common human being.

- **Azurite** – with very similar effects as the amethyst, this crystal is mostly used to help clear your mind of all negative energies that can stop one's spiritual understanding of the world before common perception.

- **Moonstone** – this wonderful crystal is most commonly used in meditations because it has the power to improve what is called "emotional vision", which can be used whenever we want to make an important decision that concerns one or more aspects of our future.

- **Lapis Lazuli** – just as it was said before, Lapis Lazuli is the "Third Eye Opener" and it can be used in a wide range of healing processes.

- **Tumbled Indigo** – very often, this stone is used to enhance our communication abilities (even behind the material world as we know it), and it is also helpful when we want to decode or give meaning to the images that we are given in our dreams or, in some cases, nightmares.

- **Turquoise** – being considered sacred in various ancient cultures, turquoise has a beneficial effect on one's spiritual growth, and it gives further understanding of the ways in which the physical and spiritual levels of the universe interact.

## *How to Develop your Intuition?*

Developing your intuition might be a little more problematic especially if you are in the initial phase of crystal healing, or if you have never experienced their beneficial effects before. But, with patience, determination, and the right information, anyone can work to improve the way in which they position themselves in this world, and find a method to have a clearer understanding of everything surrounding them – always keeping their Third Eye opened. And the most effective way to achieve this is by following some steps (which, at this point, should already be familiar to you):

1. Cleansing the crystals that are to be used – in order to make them ready for the future practice (for more information about this step, return to the second chapter).

2. Charging the crystal – because you will need to use it for very precise goals, it is necessary to make sure that the stone has enough "battery", that it is prepared to support you in the healing process; you can do that by leaving the stone either in the sunlight or under the moonlight (according to the special characteristics of the crystal) for a whole day/night.

3. Programming the crystal – this is the moment when you fill the stone with the positive thoughts that are to be of use for your purpose; for more information, go back to the subchapters dedicated to "Programming" and "Affirmations".

4. Find an effective way to use the crystal – as an amulet that you can have on you wherever you go, use it during your meditations, place it in a corner of your room (or the place you need the most), or put it under your pillow and let it work its powers on you while you sleep.

***

Receive e-mail updates on new book releases and free book promotions from Tabitha Zalot. By visiting the link below

**http://bit.ly/bonus_zalot_cs**

# Conclusion

Besides of its extremely long history, in which it has been practiced by so many diverse cultures, crystal healing is, in our times, somewhat of a taboo subject: even though it is practiced by a high percentage of the world population, not too many people are willing to admit it openly, out of fear of being criticized, or even made fun of by those who cannot accept a different perspective than theirs.

The fact that the common tendency of our century is to impose a certain way of living (and of thinking!) on everyone, is or should be widely known, but this is not the right time and place to discuss it (even though it seems like some people still need further clarifications about all the criticism that has been focused lately on the area of crystal healing). What is important is that those who embrace this way of living are aware of all the proofs and documentation that have been made over time.

Of course, as it was also mentioned throughout the book, we encourage crystal healing only in what concerns our emotional, mental, and spiritual needs. It is essential to be able to make a distinction between serious health conditions, which can be solved only through the traditional medical system, and various imbalances within the subtle body.

I hope this book was able to help inform you about crystal healing; what this type of medicine actually refers to and how it can help you reach higher levels of spirituality, establish the necessary balance of your emotions, and clear your mind in order to make room for new, more positive energies. Our intention was to give you a brief description of its background, to introduce you to the basic techniques that you will need while practicing for yourself, and to give you specific information about the ways in which crystals can help you reduce stress, anxiety, and develop your intuition.

The next step is, obviously, to try everything that you have learned from this book. This is the only way in which you will be able to convince yourself of how many beneficial effects this practice can bring to you.

Thank you again for buying this book!

Finally, if you enjoyed this book, then I'd like to ask you for a favor, would you be kind enough to leave a review for this book on Amazon? It'd be greatly appreciated!

Thank you and good luck!

*** 

Receive e-mail updates on new book releases and free book promotions from Tabitha Zalot. By visiting the link below

**http://bit.ly/bonus_zalot_cs**

***

# Check Out My Other Books

You will find these books by simply searching for them on Amazon.com

By learning how to unlock your chakras, you will even learn how to prevent diseases. Sound good so far...? Well, why don't you just go ahead and buy your own copy of this book right now? And let's get started with the 7 major chakras and their meanings.

What Reiki healing represents and how it can change your life - The benefits and advantages of Reiki - How to become a Reiki Master - What are the principles, symbols, and techniques of Reiki healing and how they work - How Reiki works on physical, mental, emotional, and spiritual levels - What does a Reiki session involve - And much, much more.

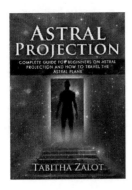

Inside this book you will learn how you too can travel through the Astral World and perform an Astral Projection. When you read this book you will be guided, step-by-step, through the process of Astral Projection, and I will help you create the best possible circumstances for achieving your goal of an Astral Travel today.

Are You Tired of Feeling Depressed, Stressed, Angry, or Anxious? This book will show you how to get rid of all of your negative feelings in a healthy, natural way. The ancient art of mindfulness can yield immediate results even for people who have never tried it before.

Take a journey all the way to the past, and witness some of the greatest moments in history, read people's auras, and see what happening hundreds of thousands of miles away is. All of that is possible through clairvoyance, and you can find out how to do that by reading this book.

You're about to discover that psychic abilities are not just a taboo myth we heard and feared ever since, but a real fact we should deal with, instead of asking ourselves questions. And because this is not that simple as it seems, this book is going to help you discover and develop your inner psychic abilities and intuition through simple exercises for beginners.

# FREE BONUS!

As a special thank you I offer you a free

TABITHA ZALOT box set.

This box set contains three life changing e-books
and one audiobook.

This is the ultimate box set for anyone committed to know
more about the concept of New Age, or anyone interested in
Meditation and Mindfulness as a way to create the life, love
and happiness you always dreamt about!

Get your copy here: **bit.ly/bonus_zalot_cs**

# Greetings from the Lean Stone Publishing Company

We want to thank you so much for reading this book to the end. We are committed to creating life changing books in the Self Help area, such as this one that you just read.

If you liked this book and want to follow us for more information on upcoming book launches, free promotions and special offers, then follow us on Facebook and Twitter!

Sign up for e-mail updates on new releases and free promotions by visiting this link:

**http://bit.ly/list_lsp_cs**

Like us: **www.facebook.com/leanstonepublishing**

Follow: **@leanstonebooks**

Thank you again for reading to the end, it means the world to us!

Made in the USA
Coppell, TX
08 December 2021